JESUS
THE MAN BEHIND THE STORIES

THE GATHERING PLACE SERIES
A project guided by Daryl L. Smith

The Gathering Place: a series of books for people interested in exploring faith issues in a non-threatening setting. Each book uses questions, Bible selections, discussion, and group service as means for this exploration.

Don•Q•Dox: a resource-creation label of The Orlando Fellowship—
an incarnational, missional-ministry community.
  Don•Q—The fictional knight *Don Quixote* (Miguel de Cervantes, 1605), whose most famous adventure includes meeting the tavern prostitute Aldonza and calling her to become the beautiful Dulcinea.
  •Dox—Documents/tools/vehicles for discovery.

As the name implies, we are on a quest to discover life as it was meant to be and invite others to join that quest. We believe that God's image is planted deeply within each of us, but most times we cannot hear the call of the "impossible dream" without the company of others who can see in us things we don't see in ourselves.

JESUS
THE MAN BEHIND THE STORIES

An 8-week Guide for Discussion and Service Groups

DARYL L. SMITH

RESOURCE *Publications* • Eugene, Oregon

JESUS—THE MAN BEHIND THE STORIES
An 8-week Guide for Discussion and Service Groups

Copyright © 2013 by Daryl L. Smith. All rights reserved. Except for brief quotations in critical publications or reviews, no part of this book may be reproduced in any manner without prior written permission from the publisher. Write: Permissions, Wipf and Stock Publishers, 199 W. 8th Ave., Suite 3, Eugene, OR 97401.

Scripture quotations mared MSG are taken from *The Message*, copyright © 1993, 1994, 1995, 1996, 2000, 2001, 2002. Used by permission of NavPress Publishing Group. All rights reserved.

Scripture quotations mared NLT are taken from the Holy Bible, New Living Translation, copyright © 1996, 2004, 2007 by Tyndale House Foundation. Used by permission of Tyndale House Publishers, Inc., Carol Stream, Illinois 60188. All rights reserved.

Resource Publications
A Division of Wipf and Stock Publishers
199 W. 8th Ave., Suite 3
Eugene, OR 97401

www.wipfandstock.com

ISBN 13: 978-1-62032-913-9

Interior Design: Carolyn B. Smith

Special thanks to **Adam Lind, Andrea Linton, Richard Smith, Susan Solano** and **Brian Taylor,** members of CL613—Recuiting and Equipping Laity, at Asbury Theological Seminary–Florida in the Spring of 2011. Additional thanks to **Rich Gilrane**, who contributed his profound theological thinking and writing.

CONTENTS

Welcome to the Group 1

Session 1: An Amazing Birth 3
(Luke 1:26–35; Matthew 1:18–25; Luke 2:1–20; Matthew 2:1–12)

Session 2: Discovering His Identity... 9
(Matthew 3:13–17; Matthew 4:1–11)

Session 3: In the Party Scene 14
(John 2:1–11; Mark 2:15–17; John 10:10)

Session 4: Fixing Brokenness 19
(Mark 1:40–45; John 8:1–11)

Session 5: Power Turned Upside Down 25
(Matthew 20:20–28; John 13:1–17)

Session 6: Facing Death Straight On 32
(Mark 14:32–36, 41–42; Luke 22:47–51; Mark 14:53–59;
Mark 15:1–15; Matt. 27:27–31; Mark 15:22–39; Matt. 27:57–61)

Session 7: Resurrected! 40
(Luke 24:1–12)

Session 8: The Call to an Impossible Mission 45
(Matthew 4:18–22; Acts 1:1–11; Acts 2:1–21)

We Serve Together 53

Group Leader Notes 55

WELCOME TO THE GROUP

The idea of sitting down with a group of people to talk about the Bible and life may scare you spitless. But relax. This group is a safe place to share your thoughts, concerns, joys, insights and doubts.

This book was created to help you take a peek behind what you've heard about the person of Jesus. Millions of pages have been written about who Jesus may or may not be. Our plan is to consider the writings of people who actually lived with Jesus—who walked on this planet when Jesus walked here, ate meals beside him and trekked the dusty roads in his shadow. Those people recorded the first four "books" of what we call the "New Testament" (part of the Bible). And those witnesses know best.

Each session includes open-ended questions, a study of the Bible, and ideas for introspection. You are free to share what you're comfortable with—and no more.

A CHANCE TO MAKE A DIFFERENCE

One highlight of these sessions is the chance to SERVE. Each session ends by asking each group member to consider choosing a "mission for the week"—a chance to make a difference in someone's life. In addition, the group will seek out opportunities to serve together, at least one time, in the community.

TO THE GROUP LEADER:

Welcome to a different kind of Bible discussion resource. This isn't about learning facts or memorizing verses. It's about studying the Bible in community (where learning works best). This study is created to connect three stories: your story, God's story and my story. Lives are transformed at that juncture.

Each session concludes with directions to help group attendees move into service—**another unique feature of this study**. Every healthy group will include study, group-member care and mission (serving others who are not group members).

Please take time to read through the "Leader Notes" at the back, where you'll find important ideas for your role as group leader. You will facilitate and guide during the coming weeks. Also, look over the "We Serve Together" ideas in the back of the book. Begin introducing the plan to serve together at the very first session.

SESSION 1—
AN AMAZING BIRTH

THE BIG IDEA:

This was a wild and crazy birth—not something you could ever create for a novel. Two books of the Bible—one written by Luke (a doctor who hung out with the people who followed Jesus) and another by Matthew (one of Jesus' closest followers; a tax collector committed to keeping good records)—give us richly different perspectives of the story behind Jesus' birth.

If we're ever to discover the real Jesus, we've got to set ourselves down in his culture, in his time, and view what was going on. Once we begin to understand his life on earth, we may be able to make some application to our here and now; to see who and what this Jesus is about in our complex world.

OPEN:
1. What is your earliest childhood memory? How far back can you remember? Is it truly a memory or have you just been told the story so many times, you think you remember it?

READ AND APPLY:

> In these longer Bible readings, group members may want to read parts silently or take turns reading out loud.

Luke 1:26–35 (MSG)
26-28In the sixth month of Elizabeth's pregnancy, God sent the angel Gabriel to the Galilean village of Nazareth to a virgin engaged to be married to a man descended from David. His name was Joseph, and the virgin's name,

Mary. Upon entering, Gabriel greeted her: Good morning! You're beautiful with God's beauty, Beautiful inside and out! God be with you.

²⁹⁻³³She was thoroughly shaken, wondering what was behind a greeting like that. But the angel assured her, "Mary, you have nothing to fear. God has a surprise for you: You will become pregnant and give birth to a son and call his name Jesus. He will be great, be called 'Son of the Highest.' The Lord God will give him the throne of his father David; He will rule Jacob's house forever—no end, ever, to his kingdom."

³⁴Mary said to the angel, "But how? I've never slept with a man."

³⁵The angel answered, The Holy Spirit will come upon you, the power of the Highest hover over you; Therefore, the child you bring to birth will be called Holy, Son of God.

Matthew 1:18–25 (MSG)

¹⁸⁻¹⁹The birth of Jesus took place like this. His mother, Mary, was engaged to be married to Joseph. Before they came to the marriage bed, Joseph discovered she was pregnant. (It was by the Holy Spirit, but he didn't know that.) Joseph, chagrined but noble, determined to take care of things quietly so Mary would not be disgraced.

²⁰⁻²³While he was trying to figure a way out, he had a dream. God's angel spoke in the dream: "Joseph, son of David, don't hesitate to get married. Mary's pregnancy is Spirit-conceived. God's Holy Spirit has made her pregnant. She will bring a son to birth, and when she does, you, Joseph, will name him Jesus—'God saves'—because he will save his people from their sins." This would bring the prophet's embryonic sermon to full term: Watch for this—a virgin will get pregnant and bear a son; They will name him Immanuel (Hebrew for "God is with us").

²⁴⁻²⁵Then Joseph woke up. He did exactly what God's angel commanded in the dream: He married Mary. But he did not consummate the marriage until she had the baby. He named the baby Jesus.

Luke 2:1–20 (MSG)

¹⁻⁵About that time Caesar Augustus ordered a census to be taken throughout the Empire. This was the first census when Quirinius was governor of Syria. Everyone had to travel to his own ancestral hometown to be accounted for. So Joseph went from the Galilean town of Nazareth up to Bethlehem in Judah, David's town, for the census. As a descendant of David, he had to go there. He went with Mary, his fiancée, who was pregnant.

⁶⁻⁷While they were there, the time came for her to give birth. She gave birth to a son, her firstborn. She wrapped him in a blanket and laid him in a manger, because there was no room in the hostel.

⁸⁻¹²There were sheepherders camping in the neighborhood. They had set night watches over their sheep. Suddenly, God's angel stood among them and God's glory blazed around them. They were terrified. The angel said, "Don't be afraid. I'm here to announce a great and joyful event that is meant for everybody, worldwide: A Savior has just been born in David's town, a Savior who is Messiah and Master. This is what you're to look for: a baby wrapped in a blanket and lying in a manger."

¹³⁻¹⁴At once the angel was joined by a huge angelic choir singing God's praises: Glory to God in the heavenly heights, Peace to all men and women on earth who please him.

¹⁵⁻¹⁸As the angel choir withdrew into heaven, the sheepherders talked it over. "Let's get over to Bethlehem as fast as we can and see for ourselves what God has revealed to us." They left, running, and found Mary and Joseph, and the baby lying in the manger. Seeing was believing. They told everyone they met what the angels had said about this child. All who heard the sheepherders were impressed.

¹⁹⁻²⁰Mary kept all these things to herself, holding them dear, deep within herself. The sheepherders returned and let loose, glorifying and praising God for everything they had heard and seen. It turned out exactly the way they'd been told!

Matthew 2:1–12 (MSG)

¹⁻²After Jesus was born in Bethlehem village, Judah territory—this was during Herod's kingship—a band of scholars arrived in Jerusalem from the East. They asked around, "Where can we find and pay homage to the newborn King of the Jews? We observed a star in the eastern sky that signaled his birth. We're on pilgrimage to worship him."

³⁻⁴When word of their inquiry got to Herod, he was terrified—and not Herod alone, but most of Jerusalem as well. Herod lost no time. He gathered all the high priests and religion scholars in the city together and asked, "Where is the Messiah supposed to be born?"

⁵⁻⁶They told him, "Bethlehem, Judah territory. The prophet Micah wrote it plainly: It's you, Bethlehem, in Judah's land, no longer bringing up the rear. From you will come the leader who will shepherd-rule my people, my Israel."

⁷⁻⁸Herod then arranged a secret meeting with the scholars from the East. Pretending to be as devout as they were, he got them to tell him exactly when the birth-announcement star appeared. Then he told them the prophecy about Bethlehem, and said, "Go find this child. Leave no stone unturned. As soon as you find him, send word and I'll join you at once in your worship."

⁹⁻¹⁰Instructed by the king, they set off. Then the star appeared again, the same star they had seen in the eastern skies. It led them on until it hovered

over the place of the child. They could hardly contain themselves: They were in the right place! They had arrived at the right time!
[11] They entered the house and saw the child in the arms of Mary, his mother. Overcome, they kneeled and worshiped him. Then they opened their luggage and presented gifts: gold, frankincense, myrrh.
[12] In a dream, they were warned not to report back to Herod. So they worked out another route, left the territory without being seen, and returned to their own country.

2. Take a few moments to think through the key points of this story, and SILENTLY jot some notes.

    Then ☑ CHECK the 5 points that you think are most important for you to remember about the story.

    Share your list with the group and why those 5 points are important to you.

1.
2.
3.
4.
5.
6.
7.
8.
9.
10.

3. Which of the characters do you feel the most sorry for? Why?
   a. Mary
   b. Joseph
   c. Gabriel
   d. The scholars ("3 wise men")
   e. King Herod
   f. Herod's priests and scholars
   g. Shepherds
   h. Angels
   i. Other _____

4. If you could use a "time-machine" to fly back into history, which part of the story would you want to land in?

   What would you want to do there?

5. Imagine the dilemma that Mary and Joseph must have experienced in their hometown when her pregnancy "started to show." If they had attended your high school, how would your friends have treated them?

6. As you look back over the story sections, which part is the hardest to believe could really be true?

   What fresh insight have you gained into what Jesus might be like? How are these insights different from what you've thought or been told about Jesus previously?

7. If you were going to get to know Jesus better, what TWO additional details do you wish the authors had shared?

   a. _____

   b. _____

ACCOUNTABLE COMMUNITY:

8. What are you facing this week that you need this group to help you walk through?

9. How can they be the most help to you?
    a. Text or tweet you in 2 days.
    b. Stop by your house.
    c. Give a call.
    d. Other _____

WE SERVE:

10. Who do you know that has recently had a baby? How can you serve them this week?
    a. Call and just say "Hi."
    b. Take a meal (make sure to call ahead).
    c. Babysit an older child so parents get a break.
    d. Other _____
    _____
    _____

GROUP PRAYER:

The group leader prays for group members and the service they will perform this week.

SESSION 2—

DISCOVERING HIS IDENTITY

THE BIG IDEA

Finding out "who we are" is one of our major tasks in life. Jesus experienced the same struggle. This incident in his life describes the time when his identity came into focus—along with his mission. And it happened through a time of celebration followed by a time of testing.

The celebration was at his baptism—a time when people have water poured over their heads or are dunked to symbolize that they are following God. But this was really awkward for John, who was doing the baptizing because he believed that Jesus really was God ... so why would God need to be baptized?

The testing (sometimes called temptation) was a time when Jesus went from great proclamation of who he was to having to struggle with the most basic issues of life like hunger or the desire to be center stage. Notice that he didn't do this on purpose. The "Spirit" (God) directed him into the wilderness—and Jesus didn't know how things would turn out in the end.

Let's see how Jesus handled these encounters.

OPEN:
1. As a child, who or what did you most like to pretend to be? How did your family respond to your pretending?

READ AND APPLY:
Matthew 3:13–17 (MSG)

[13-14] Jesus then appeared, arriving at the Jordan River from Galilee. He wanted John to baptize him. John objected, "I'm the one who needs to be baptized, not you!"

[15] But Jesus insisted. "Do it. God's work, putting things right all these centuries, is coming together right now in this baptism." So John did it.

[16-17] The moment Jesus came up out of the baptismal waters, the skies opened up and he saw God's Spirit—it looked like a dove—descending and landing on him. And along with the Spirit, a voice: "This is my Son, chosen and marked by my love, delight of my life."

Matthew 4:1–11 (MSG)

[1-3] Next Jesus was taken into the wild by the Spirit for the Test. The Devil was ready to give it. Jesus prepared for the Test by fasting forty days and forty nights. That left him, of course, in a state of extreme hunger, which the Devil took advantage of in the first test: "Since you are God's Son, speak the word that will turn these stones into loaves of bread."

[4] Jesus answered by quoting Deuteronomy: "It takes more than bread to stay alive. It takes a steady stream of words from God's mouth."

[5-6] For the second test the Devil took him to the Holy City. He sat him on top of the Temple and said, "Since you are God's Son, jump." The Devil goaded him by quoting Psalm 91: "He has placed you in the care of angels. They will catch you so that you won't so much as stub your toe on a stone."

[7] Jesus countered with another citation from Deuteronomy: "Don't you dare test the Lord your God."

[8-9] For the third test, the Devil took him to the peak of a huge mountain. He gestured expansively, pointing out all the earth's kingdoms, how glorious they all were. Then he said, "They're yours—lock, stock, and barrel. Just go down on your knees and worship me, and they're yours."

[10] Jesus' refusal was curt: "Beat it, Satan!" He backed his rebuke with a third quotation from Deuteronomy: "Worship the Lord your God, and only him. Serve him with absolute single-heartedness."

[11] The Test was over. The Devil left. And in his place, angels! Angels came and took care of Jesus' needs.

2. If you had been caught in the crowd watching Jesus' baptism, what would you have told your friends when you got home?
   a. Guess who I saw today?
   b. Hey, I just saw the coolest baptism ever!
   c. John said Jesus is God, but he baptized him anyway.
   d. I don't understand this dunking-people-in-water stuff.
   e. Other _____

3. Why do you think the appearance of the "dove" and the voice from heaven were so important for Jesus?

4. After Jesus was baptized, he fasted (ate no food) 40 days in the desert. How do you think that "prepared" him for the test he was about to face?
   a. Beats me. I'd never do that!
   b. Maybe it cleared his body and his mind.
   c. Wouldn't fasting make him *less*, not more, prepared?
   d. It helped him focus on his mission (vocation).
   e. It showed he was in control of himself.
   f. Other _____

5. Imagine that you had been "camping" with Jesus for those 40 days in the wild, what would you have done FIRST when the Devil showed up?

6. The Devil first tested Jesus by offering him food (turn stones into bread). Why do you think Jesus resisted?
   a. He wanted to show who was in charge.
   b. He realized that the Devil was trying to "mess with his head" through his stomach.
   c. Jesus didn't think he could do it. Whoever heard of turning rocks into bread, anyway?
   d. Jesus knew what was most important—God's words were like food to him.
   e. Other _____

7. What was the point of the Devil's second test?
   a. It was a playground dare.
   b. He tempted Jesus to show off.
   c. It was a good chance for him to see angels.
   d. The Devil wanted to show Jesus that he knew the Bible too.
   e. Other _____

8. The Devil's third test required Jesus to bow down and worship him. What grabs you most about Jesus' response?
   a. He was ticked off.
   b. Jesus would only worship God.
   c. Jesus already owned all of those kingdoms.
   d. Other _____

9. Coming right after his baptism, how might the tests in the wild have helped to broaden Jesus' discovery of who he was, what his life's mission was?

10. If a voice came out of the sky to speak about your worth, your personal identity, what would you want to hear said?
    _____
    _____
    _____

ACCOUNTABLE COMMUNITY:

11. What "test" (or temptation) in your life have you handled well? What did you learn about yourself from it?

    What, if anything, did you learn about God from it?

12. To which of the three tests do you think you're probably most susceptible? Why?

    How can this group help you handle a difficult test this week?

WE SERVE:

13. How will you serve someone this week who is struggling with their value as a person?
    a. Call them on the phone.
    b. Send them a text.
    c. Stop by their work.
    d. Other _____

GROUP PRAYER:

What other situations should the group pray about now and this week?

Ask for one or two volunteers to pray for specific needs. You can pray something like, "Dear God this is (your name), I ask for you to meet the need of (name of person). Amen."

The group leader closes the session by praying for group members and the service they will perform this week.

SESSION 3–

IN THE PARTY SCENE

THE BIG IDEA

Jesus spent enough time at parties and celebrations that his critics called him "a glutton and a drunkard" (see Luke 7:34). While he was dead serious about guiding people into God's ways, he was often found at the center of the party. He knew that life was to be celebrated and that eating together was a great place to share the truth of that life.

However, most events he attended were not the typical places that religious leaders would go. The banquet guests were the "non religious" of his culture—so the critics showed up to do just that ... criticize.

This session looks at two stories. One is where Jesus performed his first miracle—at a party of course. Well, actually a wedding feast. The second is a banquet at the home of one of his followers (a former tax-collector; one of those people we all love to hate).

OPEN:
1. If your friends threw a party for you on your next birthday, what would you want the room to smell like when you walked in?

READ AND APPLY:
John 2:1–11 (MSG)

[1-3] Three days later there was a wedding in the village of Cana in Galilee. Jesus' mother was there. Jesus and his disciples were guests also. When they started running low on wine at the wedding banquet, Jesus' mother told him, "They're just about out of wine."

[4] Jesus said, "Is that any of our business, Mother—yours or mine? This isn't my time. Don't push me."

[5] She went ahead anyway, telling the servants, "Whatever he tells you, do it."

[6-7] Six stoneware water pots were there, used by the Jews for ritual washings. Each held twenty to thirty gallons. Jesus ordered the servants, "Fill the pots with water." And they filled them to the brim.

[8] "Now fill your pitchers and take them to the host," Jesus said, and they did.

[9-10] When the host tasted the water that had become wine (he didn't know what had just happened but the servants, of course, knew), he called out to the bridegroom, "Everybody I know begins with their finest wines and after the guests have had their fill brings in the cheap stuff. But you've saved the best till now!"

[11] This act in Cana of Galilee was the first sign Jesus gave, the first glimpse of his glory. And his disciples believed in him.

Mark 2:15–17 (MSG)
Later Jesus and his disciples were at home [Levi's, also called Matthew, house] having supper with a collection of disreputable guests. Unlikely as it seems, more than a few of them had become followers. The religion scholars and Pharisees saw him keeping this kind of company and lit into his disciples: "What kind of example is this, acting cozy with the riffraff?" Jesus, overhearing, shot back, "Who needs a doctor: the healthy or the sick? I'm here inviting the sin-sick, not the spiritually-fit."

> On another day, as Jesus' critics were again accusing him of partying too much, he lays the truth out for all to hear. This is one of his most profound statements about life. Imagine how the religious leaders liked being called thieves. He said,

The thief's purpose is to steal and kill and destroy. My purpose is to give them a rich and satisfying life. [John 10:10, NLT]

2. If you were one of the wedding servers in the first story, what would you have said when Jesus sent you to fill a pot with water?
   a. Yeah, right after I'm done picking the lint out of my navel.
   b. Have you ever tried to pick up one of these monsters?
   c. If you say so, but I don't know who you think you are.
   d. Other _____

3. As a party guest, what would surprise you about the interaction between Jesus and his mother?
   a. In a male-dominated culture, his mother told him what to do.
   b. Jesus acted like he didn't really care to help.
   c. Jesus, as a guest, started ordering people around.
   d. Jesus seemed like he wanted to avoid the spotlight.
   e. Other _____

4. In the second story, Levi, as a tax collector, was probably not surprised at being called "riffraff," but if you weren't used to this kind of name-calling, what would your gut response have been to the religious leaders?
   a. Let Jesus handle it.
   b. Punch them out.
   c. "Hey, don't lump me in with this crowd."
   d. Team up with the other disciples and...
   e. Other _____

5. Why do you think Jesus didn't seem to worry about his reputation?

   How could he so easily mix with so many different kinds of people?

6. Of the two parties, which would you have felt most comfortable attending? Why?

7. What kind of social setting bores you to tears? What social setting fires you up?

8. If you could invite ANYONE in the world to your party, who would be the top 2 on your "top 10" list?

_____

_____

Where would Jesus be on your list? Why?

ACCOUNTABLE COMMUNITY:

9. If you were emailing a friend about what you've discovered from these stories, how would you describe what Jesus meant by "a rich and satisfying life"?

10. What do you think Jesus' "rich and satisfying life" might mean for you? How can this group help you take the next best steps toward discovering it?

WE SERVE:

Who might you surprise with a "mini-party" this week? (Sending them an e-card, dropping off a balloon at work, etc.)

_____

GROUP PRAYER:

Let each person in the group pray silently for the person on their left. Remember your person's "next steps" and the service they will try to accomplish this next week.

After a minute or so, let the group leader close by praying out loud.

SESSION 4– FIXING BROKENNESS

THE BIG IDEA

Jesus made a habit of seeking out broken people, right where they were, and making them whole. And since all of us have brokenness, let's see if these "case studies" from 2000+ years ago have a fresh word for us.

In the first story, Jesus met a man with leprosy. In Jesus' time, people who suffered the disease of leprosy were cut off from their families and friends. They lived outside their city or village, often in caves. No one was allowed to touch them, so friends or family members dropped off food to keep them from starving to death. Of course, many did. They were barricaded off from everything they cared about. But, when Jesus walked by, the leper risked everything to approach—to take the chance of a lifetime. And Jesus, never bound by meaningless rules, reached out and touched him.

In another powerful scene, a woman is dragged to Jesus, supposedly caught "in adultery." Interestingly, her accusers "forgot" to bring the man she was allegedly involved with. So, we have no way of knowing whether she was actually guilty or if this was a setup to put Jesus in an impossible spot.

OPEN:
1. What's the most expensive household item you ever dropped and broke? Who did it belong to? What's the first thing you did after it crashed? (Cry? Run? Hide? Confess?)

READ AND APPLY:

Mark 1:40–45 (MSG)

⁴⁰A leper came to him, begging on his knees, "If you want to, you can cleanse me."

⁴¹⁻⁴⁵Deeply moved, Jesus put out his hand, touched him, and said, "I want to. Be clean." Then and there the leprosy was gone, his skin smooth and healthy. Jesus dismissed him with strict orders: "Say nothing to anyone. Take the offering for cleansing that Moses prescribed and present yourself to the priest. This will validate your healing to the people." But as soon as the man was out of earshot, he told everyone he met what had happened, spreading the news all over town. So Jesus kept to out-of-the-way places, no longer able to move freely in and out of the city. But people found him, and came from all over.

2. If you've ever been desperate enough to beg for help, you know the humiliation this leper felt. What do you think was the most important thing Jesus did to begin the leper's healing?
   a. Spoke kindly to him.
   b. Was "deeply moved"—demonstrated that he truly cared about the man's plight.
   c. Gave the gift of human touch (how many years had it been since he'd felt another person's skin?).
   d. Healing the outer sickness first so the inner scars could begin to heal.
   e. Other _____

3. You are the leper. Imagine what that touch from Jesus hand must have felt like, what it did for your whole being after those years of isolation. What 5 words come to your mind to express the feeling?

_____ _____ _____

_____ _____

John 8:1–11 (MSG)

¹⁻²Jesus went across to Mount Olives, but he was soon back in the Temple again. Swarms of people came to him. He sat down and taught them. ³⁻⁶The religion scholars and Pharisees led in a woman who had been caught in an act of adultery. They stood her in plain sight of everyone and said, "Teacher, this woman was caught red-handed in the act of adultery. Moses, in the Law, gives orders to stone such persons. What do you say?" They were trying to trap him into saying something incriminating so they could bring charges against him.

⁶⁻⁸Jesus bent down and wrote with his finger in the dirt. They kept at him, badgering him. He straightened up and said, "The sinless one among you, go first: Throw the stone." Bending down again, he wrote some more in the dirt.

⁹⁻¹⁰Hearing that, they walked away, one after another, beginning with the oldest. The woman was left alone. Jesus stood up and spoke to her. "Woman, where are they? Does no one condemn you?"

¹¹"No one, Master."

"Neither do I," said Jesus. "Go on your way. From now on, don't sin."

4. Suppose you were authoring a daily blog and stumbled upon this street scene with Jesus, the rock-carrying men, and this woman. How would you title tomorrow's post?

   _____

   If you had stayed long enough to watch the men walk away, what 3 key points would you want to share with your readers?

   a. _____

   b. _____

   c. _____

21

5. If you're a MALE, what role would you have played in this story?
   a. Tried to hide in a doorway.
   b. Gotten a really big rock to give her what she deserved.
   c. Gone looking for "her man."
   d. Tried to protect her from the crazies.
   e. Other _____

   If you're a FEMALE, what role would you have played in this story?
   a. Cheered on the men who were enforcing the law.
   b. Screamed in horror.
   c. Run to protect my family.
   d. Tried to get the woman help from someone nearby.
   e. Other _____

6. This fragile woman's life is in grave danger. Why do you think Jesus took time to write a note in the sand?
   a. To take control of the chaos.
   b. To try to think up a good answer.
   c. To let the men reflect on their own wrongs.
   d. To write a note that would accuse all her accusers.
   e. Other _____

7. If you had been Jesus, what would you have written in the dirt? Put some of those thoughts in the sand below. After a few minutes, share with the group what you've written.

ACCOUNTABLE COMMUNITY:

8. What is the best news from these two stories for you? Why?
9. How would you like Jesus to show up in your life and bring wholeness to a brokenness?

    How can this group help you in that healing?

WE SERVE:

10. Think about someone you will encounter (at work, shopping, home or neighborhood) who needs a healing act or word from you.

    Who is it and what will you do to serve them this week?

    _____
    _____
    _____

GROUP PRAYER:

Let 3 or 4 people volunteer to pray for specific group needs.

When they have prayed, all group members close their eyes so each can focus on the words as the group leader speaks this blessing (a blessing is an encouraging word from God):

> *"As you go out this week, may you begin to discover healing for the brokenness you carry. May your service be life-transforming for the person you share it with. And may you know God's peace surrounding all you do."*

SESSION 5—

POWER TURNED UPSIDE-DOWN

THE BIG IDEA

Jesus was never about seeking job titles or positions. The Bible tells us that he gave all that up when he moved from being just God to become both God and a human. We don't understand how all that works, but we can read what Jesus said and see how he lived. Through that life on Earth he personified serving; and serving always gets lived out in terms of bringing God's justice to every injustice.

Yet, as we read the Bible, it appears that his closest followers had trouble grasping the serving concept, even after three years of interning with him.

One day as Jesus and his group of 12 followers (disciples) traveled toward Jerusalem (the capital city), he knew that he was walking into a pit of evil. He knew his remaining teaching time was limited because he would be killed. So as they walked together, he reviewed some of his most vital teachings—to make sure his disciples truly grasped what they'd been taught.

Right in the middle of the discussion, the mother of two of his followers stepped up to ask for special privilege for her sons. We'll see how all that plays out and how the other disciples responded.

A few days later, on the night he is arrested, the night before he was killed, Jesus made one last attempt to demonstrate the life he'd called his followers to. But this time he didn't just talk. He gave them an object lesson—he took the role of a servant and washed their feet. As you can imagine, they were embarrassed, as they finally started to get the point.

It seems that when we are striving for power and position, people get run over. When we are committed to serving, others' needs are met at all levels and in all situations.

OPEN:

1. Who was your favorite elementary school teacher? Can you remember his/her name? What makes them memorable?

READ AND APPLY:
Matthew 20:20–28 (MSG)
[20]*It was about that time that the mother of the Zebedee brothers came with her two sons and knelt before Jesus with a request.*
[21]*"What do you want?" Jesus asked.*

She said, "Give your word that these two sons of mine will be awarded the highest places of honor in your kingdom, one at your right hand, one at your left hand."
[22]*Jesus responded, "You have no idea what you're asking." And he said to James and John, "Are you capable of drinking the cup that I'm about to drink?"*

They said, "Sure, why not?"
[23]*Jesus said, "Come to think of it, you are going to drink my cup. But as to awarding places of honor, that's not my business. My Father is taking care of that."*
[24-28]*When the ten others heard about this, they lost their tempers, thoroughly disgusted with the two brothers. So Jesus got them together to settle things down. He said, "You've observed how godless rulers throw their weight around, how quickly a little power goes to their heads. It's not going to be that way with you. Whoever wants to be great must become a servant. Whoever wants to be first among you must be your slave. That is what the Son of Man has done: He came to serve, not be served—and then to give away his life in exchange for the many who are held hostage."*

2. As an "invisible disciple," imagine you're walking along with Jesus, as his teaching seems to get really "heavy"—suspenseful. You know something's up as you hang on every word. When James's and John's mamma interrupts asking for special favors for her boys, what sensation starts to run through you?

3. As you read how Jesus uses this teachable moment to explain the life of serving instead of grasping for power, what story from your own experience comes to mind? When have you seen true serving modeled—or maybe the opposite?

> Now read this next Bible section using THREE readers: a narrator, Jesus and Peter.

John 13:1–17 (MSG)

¹⁻²*Just before the Passover Feast, Jesus knew that the time had come to leave this world to go to the Father. Having loved his dear companions, he continued to love them right to the end. It was suppertime. The Devil by now had Judas, son of Simon the Iscariot, firmly in his grip, all set for the betrayal.*

³⁻⁶*Jesus knew that the Father had put him in complete charge of everything, that he came from God and was on his way back to God. So he got up from the supper table, set aside his robe, and put on an apron. Then he poured water into a basin and began to wash the feet of the disciples, drying them with his apron. When he got to Simon Peter, Peter said, "Master, you wash my feet?"*

⁷*Jesus answered, "You don't understand now what I'm doing, but it will be clear enough to you later."*

⁸*Peter persisted, "You're not going to wash my feet—ever!"*

Jesus said, "If I don't wash you, you can't be part of what I'm doing."

⁹*"Master!" said Peter. "Not only my feet, then. Wash my hands! Wash my head!"*

¹⁰⁻¹²*Jesus said, "If you've had a bath in the morning, you only need your feet*

washed now and you're clean from head to toe. My concern, you understand, is holiness, not hygiene. So now you're clean. But not every one of you." (He knew who was betraying him. That's why he said, "Not every one of you.") After he had finished washing their feet, he took his robe, put it back on, and went back to his place at the table.

¹²⁻¹⁷Then he said, "Do you understand what I have done to you? You address me as 'Teacher' and 'Master,' and rightly so. That is what I am. So if I, the Master and Teacher, washed your feet, you must now wash each other's feet. I've laid down a pattern for you. What I've done, you do. I'm only pointing out the obvious. A servant is not ranked above his master; an employee doesn't give orders to the employer. If you understand what I'm telling you, act like it—and live a blessed life."

4. What most impresses you about how Jesus handled this awkward situation, when a servant didn't show up to do the expected foot washing?
   a. He didn't order someone to find the servant.
   b. He didn't announce that he was going to wash their feet, he just started.
   c. He didn't get sick handling dirty feet.
   d. He gently answered Peter's questions without embarrassing him.
   e. Other _____

5. Look at the three phrases in John 13:3 that describe Jesus. They seem to be critical to his ability to become a servant.

   How do you think each "truth statement" affected his ability/willingness to serve? (What's the principle?)

   How would you translate each phrase into a statement about yourself?

   • "...in complete charge of everything":

   Jesus: _____

   You: _____

- "he came from God"

Jesus: _____

You: _____

- "was on his way back to God"

Jesus: _____

You: _____

6. *Social justice* is a term that describes how we put Jesus' teaching about "serving" vs. "taking" into practical terms. It's the idea of applying God's justice to every social setting. Think about how you might apply this concept in your everyday world. Jot a few notes below to describe how living a "social justice life" might impact your responses to "hard" situations, like:

    a. Poor or homeless people

    b. Family members who want too much attention

    c. People of a different race or ethnic group

    d. People who are in a different age grouping than you

e. People who belong to a different political group than you

f. Other difficult situations _____

ACCOUNTABLE COMMUNITY:

7. If Jesus showed up at your work or school to take you to lunch, how do you think the conversation would go?

   What would you laugh about, because you screwed up?

   What area of life might he want to talk seriously about?

   What next steps do you think Jesus would ask you to take?

WE SERVE:

8. Now again we have the chance to practice what we've been studying. What person or situation have you seen that needed to be served, but you've been working really hard to avoid? Is this the week to do something?

   _____

   _____

   _____

GROUP PRAYER:

Form a prayer huddle in the middle of the room.

Starting with the person to the left of the group leader, let each person pray a ONE SENTENCE prayer. Go around the circle until all have prayed.

If ANYONE is UNCOMFORTABLE praying out loud, they can just say "Pass" when it's their turn. Or they can pray silently and say "Done" when they have finished.

SESSION 6–
FACING DEATH STRAIGHT ON

THE BIG IDEA

Perhaps life's biggest mystery is what happens to us at the end. At best we misunderstand death; at worst, we fear it. Jesus faced death head on ... not that he looked forward to it. He didn't. However, he never backed down, even when it meant torture.

Yet greater than one man's death is the biggest picture of all. Jesus death took on eternal significance.

To help us understand why Jesus death was so vital, consider this: Have you ever tried a "do it yourself" job without the right tools? Maybe, lacking a hammer, you drove a nail with the butt end of a screwdriver. Maybe it even sort of worked—but there were consequences. At the least, it took a lot longer—and likely you dented the surrounding surface ... and maybe even broke your screwdriver!

Things—including us—are made for a specific use! In our case, the purpose is a life lived with and dependent upon God. But in the ultimate attempt at a "do it yourself" project, we try to live apart from that purpose and relationship. It's not a new problem. In fact, it started with the first man and woman—who once had known the joy of walking with God, but decided to go it alone. The consequence? They ended up hiding, naked and fearful, as their Creator called to them across Paradise.

This going it alone—this attempt to "do it yourself"—is what the Bible calls sin. Sin has consequences! But these consequences shouldn't be understood as the vengeful acts of an angry God. Rather, they are the objectively unavoidable consequences of using our lives for a purpose other than we were designed for—just like using a screwdriver to drive a nail!

In fact, God prefers that we not suffer these consequences! His very first acts toward the rebellion of that first woman and man were merciful—continuing to call them and fashioning clothing for their protection. As history unfolded, God continued a relentless pursuit of reconciliation by instituting a sacrificial system, in which sin was atoned for (others standing in for us sinners) so that relationship could be continually offered.

Finally, when God knew humans were ready to hear the full story, God became human in Jesus the Christ—offering the ultimate, once-and-for-all atoning sacrifice in himself. Jesus, who had ultimate power at his command, endured the consequences of the sins of others on the cross—and from the cross even offered forgiveness to those who tormented him!

By all rights we SHOULD be allowed to "suffer the consequences," but God simply won't give up on us! He was, is, and always will be—until the end of time—"on the cross" for us, bearing the burden of our sinfulness, and offering anew the prospect of purposeful relationship—a life according to design.

Let's see how this story unfolds!

OPEN:
1. Think back to a time when you had to watch someone "go their own way," knowing they were making big mistakes—and that they would suffer big consequences. What was the person's relationship to you? What action, if any, did you attempt, to change the person's direction?

2. Describe the first funeral you ever attended. How old were you? If you were young, what did people tell you about what was going on?

READ AND APPLY:
Mark 14:32–36; 41–42 (MSG) — In the Garden

32-34They came to an area called Gethsemane. Jesus told his disciples, "Sit here while I pray." He took Peter, James, and John with him. He plunged into a sinkhole of dreadful agony. He told them, "I feel bad enough right now to die. Stay here and keep vigil with me."

35-36Going a little ahead, he fell to the ground and prayed for a way out: "Papa, Father, you can—can't you?—get me out of this. Take this cup away from me. But please, not what I want—what do you want?"

41-42He came back... and said..."The Son of Man is about to be betrayed into the hands of sinners. Get up. Let's get going. My betrayer has arrived."

Luke 22:47–51 (MSG) — Jesus is Arrested

47-48No sooner were the words out of his mouth than a crowd showed up, Judas, the one from the Twelve, in the lead. He came right up to Jesus to kiss him. Jesus said, "Judas, you would betray the Son of Man with a kiss?"

49-50When those with him saw what was happening, they said, "Master, shall we fight?" One of them took a swing at the Chief Priest's servant and cut off his right ear.

51Jesus said, "Let them be. Even in this." Then, touching the servant's ear, he healed him.

3. Because Jesus knew certain details of what was going to happen to him (for example, that his betrayer was coming, that he would be killed), he pleaded with God for any other option. Yet he willingly went ahead with the plan, when no other option would do.

   When have you cared so much for another person that you willingly suffered trouble or pain, **that they caused**, because the relationship was so important to you?

   How did you move forward (if you did)?

Mark 14:53–59 (MSG) — Jesus before Religious Leaders

⁵³⁻⁵⁴*They led Jesus to the Chief Priest, where the high priests, religious leaders, and scholars had gathered together. Peter followed at a safe distance until they got to the Chief Priest's courtyard, where he mingled with the servants and warmed himself at the fire.*

⁵⁵⁻⁵⁹*The high priests conspiring with the Jewish Council looked high and low for evidence against Jesus by which they could sentence him to death. They found nothing. Plenty of people were willing to bring in false charges, but nothing added up, and they ended up canceling each other out. Then a few of them stood up and lied: "We heard him say, 'I am going to tear down this Temple, built by hard labor, and in three days build another without lifting a hand.'" But even they couldn't agree exactly.*

Mark 15:1–15 (MSG) — The "Trial"

¹*At dawn's first light, the high priests, with the religious leaders and scholars, arranged a conference with the entire Jewish Council. After tying Jesus securely, they took him out and presented him to Pilate.*

²⁻³*Pilate asked him, "Are you the 'King of the Jews'?"*

He answered, "If you say so." The high priests let loose a barrage of accusations.

⁴⁻⁵*Pilate asked again, "Aren't you going to answer anything? That's quite a list of accusations." Still, he said nothing. Pilate was impressed, really impressed.*

⁶⁻¹⁰*It was a custom at the Feast to release a prisoner, anyone the people asked for. There was one prisoner called Barabbas, locked up with the insurrectionists who had committed murder during the uprising against Rome. As the crowd came up and began to present its petition for him to release a prisoner, Pilate anticipated them: "Do you want me to release the King of the Jews to you?" Pilate knew by this time that it was through sheer spite that the high priests had turned Jesus over to him.*

¹¹⁻¹²*But the high priests by then had worked up the crowd to ask for the release of Barabbas. Pilate came back, "So what do I do with this man you call King of the Jews?"*

¹³*They yelled, "Nail him to a cross!"*

¹⁴*Pilate objected, "But for what crime?"*

But they yelled all the louder, "Nail him to a cross!"

¹⁵*Pilate gave the crowd what it wanted, set Barabbas free and turned Jesus over for whipping and crucifixion.*

4. Why do you think Jesus declined to defend himself in front of Pilate?

5. When the crowd chanted for Barabbas, what do you think was going through Jesus' mind?
   a. Ah, I can escape while this crowd is going crazy.
   b. When will you all understand the big picture of what I'm doing here?
   c. It can only get worse from here on.
   d. I wish God would get me out of this.
   e. Other _____

Matthew 27:27–31 (MSG) — The Soldiers' Abuse
27-31The soldiers assigned to the governor took Jesus into the governor's palace and got the entire brigade together for some fun. They stripped him and dressed him in a red toga. They plaited a crown from branches of a thornbush and set it on his head. They put a stick in his right hand for a scepter. Then they knelt before him in mocking reverence: "Bravo, King of the Jews!" they said. "Bravo!" Then they spit on him and hit him on the head with the stick. When they had had their fun, they took off the toga and put his own clothes back on him. Then they proceeded out to the crucifixion.

Mark 15:22–39 (MSG) — The Crucifixion
22-24The soldiers brought Jesus to Golgotha, meaning "Skull Hill." They offered him a mild painkiller (wine mixed with myrrh), but he wouldn't take it. And they nailed him to the cross. They divided up his clothes and threw dice to see who would get them.

25-30They nailed him up at nine o'clock in the morning. The charge against him—the king of the jews—was printed on a poster. Along with him, they crucified two criminals, one to his right, the other to his left. People passing along the road jeered, shaking their heads in mock lament: "You bragged that you could tear down the Temple and then rebuild it in three days—so show us your stuff! Save yourself! If you're really God's Son, come down from that cross!"

31-32The high priests, along with the religion scholars, were right there mixing it up with the rest of them, having a great time poking fun at him: "He saved others—but he can't save himself! Messiah, is he? King of Israel?

Then let him climb down from that cross. We'll all become believers then!" Even the men crucified alongside him joined in the mockery.

³³⁻³⁴At noon the sky became extremely dark. The darkness lasted three hours. At three o'clock, Jesus groaned out of the depths, crying loudly, "Eloi, Eloi, lama sabachthani?" which means, "My God, my God, why have you abandoned me?"

³⁵⁻³⁶Some of the bystanders who heard him said, "Listen, he's calling for Elijah." Someone ran off, soaked a sponge in sour wine, put it on a stick, and gave it to him to drink, saying, "Let's see if Elijah comes to take him down."

³⁷⁻³⁹But Jesus, with a loud cry, gave his last breath. At that moment the Temple curtain ripped right down the middle. When the Roman captain standing guard in front of him saw that he had quit breathing, he said, "This has to be the Son of God!"

6. Many people who witnessed Jesus' crucifixion used the event as an opportunity to mock and taunt him.

   Circle their comments in the verses above.

   In the space below, paraphrase their thoughts that echo similar thoughts you've had.

37

7. One bystander, the Roman captain, came to the startling realization that "this has to be the Son of God." What do you think he saw that made him make that "dangerous" proclamation?

Matthew 27:57–61 (MSG) — The Tomb

[57-61] Late in the afternoon a wealthy man from Arimathea, a disciple of Jesus, arrived. His name was Joseph. He went to Pilate and asked for Jesus' body. Pilate granted his request. Joseph took the body and wrapped it in clean linens, put it in his own tomb, a new tomb only recently cut into the rock, and rolled a large stone across the entrance. Then he went off. But Mary Magdalene and the other Mary stayed, sitting in plain view of the tomb.

8. After Jesus' crucifixion, some people theorized that he never really died. What statements in these Bible selections refute that theory?

_____
_____
_____
_____

9. Why do you think Mary Magdalene and the other Mary stayed "in view of the tomb"?
   a. They were really tired after a long day.
   b. It was the closest they could still get to a special friend.
   c. They didn't know what to do with their grief.
   d. Other _____

ACCOUNTABLE COMMUNITY:

10. Is there a part of this painful story that makes you feel more hopeful? That helps you understand Jesus better? If yes, which part? If not, why not?

11. How can this group stand with you this week?
    a. Pray
    b. Text
    c. Drop by
    d. Other _____

WE SERVE:

12. Find someone you know who is going through a time of grief (due to a significant loss):
    - Take time to let them know you care.
    - Don't counsel; just express your concern and listen as they talk.
    - Only stay for 10–15 minutes unless absolutely necessary.

GROUP PRAYER:

The group leader prays for the group members and all the people they will serve this week.

SESSION 7—
RESURRECTED!

THE BIG IDEA

When we were ready to see the full story—Jesus' life, death, and resurrection—Jesus showed us how to live with integrity and God-consciousness. Jesus showed us how to accept all the good and bad that living in a do-it-ourselves world has to offer. And most importantly, in resurrection, Jesus demonstrated the truth that God is able to suck up all of the evil of life—even to the point of his own torture and death—and convert it into something wonderful. Jesus showed us that, ultimately, even the worst we will go through is being formed into something that will eventually make us grateful it happened—although it's painful in the present.

God's intention is to redeem (transform) all of that stuff absorbed on the cross by fashioning it into an amazing resurrection of the entire creation. Thus, we can expect bad times. But just as surely we can be confident that we never go through suffering alone. We can look forward with hope and expectation.

Throughout Jesus' time on Earth, he repeatedly told his followers of God's plan—that he would be killed and come back from the dead. But, when it came right down to it, his followers were surprised when it actually happened. The reality of the resurrection took time to become reality in their minds and hearts.

OPEN:
1. When were you last offered something that seemed "too good to be true"? What was it?

2. Tell about a time when you shared a wonderful and amazing story but people didn't believe you. How did you convince them that it was true? Or did you?

READ AND APPLY:
Luke 24:1–12 (MSG)

¹⁻³*At the crack of dawn on Sunday, the women came to the tomb carrying the burial spices they had prepared. They found the entrance stone rolled back from the tomb, so they walked in. But once inside, they couldn't find the body of the Master Jesus.*

⁴⁻⁸*They were puzzled, wondering what to make of this. Then, out of nowhere it seemed, two men, light cascading over them, stood there. The women were awestruck and bowed down in worship. The men said, "Why are you looking for the Living One in a cemetery? He is not here, but raised up. Remember how he told you when you were still back in Galilee that he had to be handed over to sinners, be killed on a cross, and in three days rise up?" Then they remembered Jesus' words.*

⁹⁻¹¹*They left the tomb and broke the news of all this to the Eleven and the rest. Mary Magdalene, Joanna, Mary the mother of James, and the other women with them kept telling these things to the apostles, but the apostles didn't believe a word of it, thought they were making it all up.*

¹²*But Peter jumped to his feet and ran to the tomb. He stooped to look in and saw a few grave clothes, that's all. He walked away puzzled, shaking his head.*

3. Suppose you had walked into the garden following Jesus burial in the tomb, and not found his body there. What reaction would best describe your feelings?
    a. "Where's the body?! Call 911!"
    b. "Rejoice! Jesus is alive! Time to party!"
    c. "No Way! This is just plain crazy!"
    d. Pure shock and utter speechlessness.
    e. Other _____

4. The "men" at the tomb (actually angels) said that Jesus accomplished what he set out to do ("be handed over, crucified, and rise from the dead on the third day"). This statement must have jogged the women's memories.

   Why do you think the angels mentioned these THREE specific events? How might this have helped the women's understanding of what was happening around them?

5. The apostles (or disciples, closest followers) didn't believe the report of the women. If you were tasked with mediating between those reporting the resurrection and those who didn't believe it, what would you make sure each side understood? Jot down the "proofs" for each side of the question:

Here's why you should believe my story:

Here's why this story can't be true:

6. What person(s)/trait(s) do you most identify with in this story?
   a. The women at the tomb (concerned/then filled with a sense of urgency to tell others)
   b. The two "men" (faithful/proclaiming the news)
   c. The apostles (doubting/skeptical/having to see it for themselves)
   d. Peter (curious/awed at the scene but silent)
   e. The dead (Will you keep it down? I'm trying to sleep here!)
   f. Other _____

7. What fears do you think keep people from believing the story of Jesus' life, death and resurrection?
   a. Fear of what others may think (I'll be labeled a fool)
   b. Fear of the unknown (I can't prove this!)
   c. Fear of surrender (If this is true, I've got to do something about it … and I don't want to submit to anyone, including Jesus!)
   d. Other _____

ACCOUNTABLE COMMUNITY:

8. Both the apostles and the women harbored some skepticism about Jesus' resurrection. What about following Jesus raises your greatest doubts?

   What eases your skepticism?

9. How can this group pray for you—and journey with you so you may better experience the joy of the resurrection?

WE SERVE:

Find an excuse to celebrate with someone this week! Send flowers or a congratulations message (maybe even in person) to someone who had a baby, found a job, sold a house, finished a project, reached a goal …. If necessary, make up a reason! Give someone an experience of joy.

GROUP PRAYER:

The leader will voice each sentence of the following prayer, allowing group members to "complete the thought" silently:

Dear God:
Thank you for doing the impossible—coming back to life to conquer death. [silence]

Help us to understand how amazing that is, and what it means for us. [silence]

Thank you for telling us about people who responded to your resurrection with doubt or skepticism. [silence]

Help us, in our doubt and skepticism, to turn to you for truth and understanding. [silence]

Help us to grow in our love for you and our willingness to share your amazing story with others. [silence]

SESSION 8 – THE CALL TO AN IMPOSSIBLE MISSION

THE BIG IDEA

The Bible tells us that Jesus didn't just come to share some nice ideas, live a good life, and then leave. The Bible is really clear that Jesus was on a mission to invite all people back into a healthy relationship with God. But he didn't come to carry out the mission by himself, like some Lone Ranger. He intended to include every human—equipping everyone who would follow to help change the world. Yet, he knew it was an impossible mission unless the presence of God was powering his followers toward success.

So from the very first day of his public work, when he called his first disciples, he started planting the mission in their minds and hearts. The first part of the story (below) describes his mission call with the words "Come, follow Me, and I will make a new kind of fisherman out of you." They had no idea what that meant.

The last two parts of the story take place as Jesus is leaving earth—and several days after he left. Jesus summarizes what he had been trying to teach them for three years. Then he lets them know the secret of how they will fulfill his mission. He's leaving (as the human they've known), but his "spirit"—we use the term "Holy Spirit"—will return to dwell, not in bodily form, but in spiritual form, inside them. Try to catch this amazing transition from his first call to a few fishermen, until he launches them on an earth-restoring impossible mission.

OPEN:
1. When was the last time you were totally intimidated; you were over your head and you knew it? Describe your experience.

OR: When were you asked to perform a job or task you felt totally unqualified for? How did you get through it?

READ AND APPLY:
Matthew 4:18–22 (MSG)

[18-20] *Walking along the beach of Lake Galilee, Jesus saw two brothers: Simon (later called Peter) and Andrew. They were fishing, throwing their nets into the lake. It was their regular work. Jesus said to them, "Come with me. I'll make a new kind of fisherman out of you. I'll show you how to catch men and women instead of perch and bass." They didn't ask questions, but simply dropped their nets and followed.*

[21-22] *A short distance down the beach they came upon another pair of brothers, James and John, Zebedee's sons. These two were sitting in a boat with their father, Zebedee, mending their fishnets. Jesus made the same offer to them, and they were just as quick to follow, abandoning boat and father.*

2. If you had been the father of James and John, trying to keep your business afloat, what would you have said when a stranger came along and "commanded" your sons to drop their stuff, leave the family business, and follow him?
   a. Are you kidding me? Who's going to help me with all this work?
   b. Hey, that's Jesus. Do what he tells you.
   c. Don't be crazy, how will you support yourself?
   d. They left? Huh! I didn't notice.
   e. Other _____

3. The context of Jesus' world is different than ours, but what do you imagine there was about Jesus that made the guys want to follow him?
   a. They heard he was a star.
   b. They were sick of fishing and this was a way out.
   c. He offered a purpose they couldn't resist.
   d. Other _____

> Three years passed—three years of teaching and modeling the "missional" life—and Jesus gathers one more time with his followers (disciples). The doctor Luke, who wrote the book called Luke, is also writing the notes here.

Acts 1:1–11 (MSG)

1-5Dear Theophilus, in the first volume of this book I wrote on everything that Jesus began to do and teach until the day he said good-bye to the apostles, the ones he had chosen through the Holy Spirit, and was taken up to heaven. After his death, he presented himself alive to them in many different settings over a period of forty days. In face-to-face meetings, he talked to them about things concerning the kingdom of God. As they met and ate meals together, he told them that they were on no account to leave Jerusalem but "must wait for what the Father promised: the promise you heard from me. John baptized in water; you will be baptized in the Holy Spirit. And soon."

6When they were together for the last time they asked, "Master, are you going to restore the kingdom to Israel now? Is this the time?"

7-8He told them, "You don't get to know the time. Timing is the Father's business. What you'll get is the Holy Spirit. And when the Holy Spirit comes on you, you will be able to be my witnesses in Jerusalem, all over Judea and Samaria, even to the ends of the world."

9-11These were his last words. As they watched, he was taken up and disappeared in a cloud. They stood there, staring into the empty sky. Suddenly two men appeared—in white robes! They said, "You Galileans!—why do you just stand here looking up at an empty sky? This very Jesus who was taken up from among you to heaven will come as certainly—and mysteriously—as he left."

4. For a 40-day period after the resurrection, the followers met with Jesus many times. Now they huddled around him for one last goodbye. How would you have reported this scene for the Jerusalem TV station? What ONE question would you have asked Jesus before he left?

_____

_____

_____

> After Jesus left earth, several days passed. One day as Jesus' followers gathered together, a strange and mysterious event exploded into their lives.

Acts 2:1–21 (MSG)

[1-4] When the Feast of Pentecost came, they were all together in one place. Without warning there was a sound like a strong wind, gale force—no one could tell where it came from. It filled the whole building. Then, like a wildfire, the Holy Spirit spread through their ranks, and they started speaking in a number of different languages as the Spirit prompted them.

[5-11] There were many Jews staying in Jerusalem just then, devout pilgrims from all over the world. When they heard the sound, they came on the run. Then when they heard, one after another, their own mother tongues being spoken, they were thunderstruck. They couldn't for the life of them figure out what was going on, and kept saying, "Aren't these all Galileans? How come we're hearing them talk in our various mother tongues?"

> Parthians, Medes, and Elamites; Visitors from Mesopotamia, Judea, and Cappadocia, Pontus and Asia, Phrygia and Pamphylia, Egypt and the parts of Libya belonging to Cyrene; Immigrants from Rome, both Jews and proselytes; Even Cretans and Arabs!

"They're speaking our languages, describing God's mighty works!"

[12] Their heads were spinning; they couldn't make head or tail of any of it. They talked back and forth, confused: "What's going on here?"

[13] Others joked, "They're drunk on cheap wine."

¹⁴⁻²¹That's when Peter stood up and, backed by the other eleven, spoke out with bold urgency: "Fellow Jews, all of you who are visiting Jerusalem, listen carefully and get this story straight. These people aren't drunk as some of you suspect. They haven't had time to get drunk—it's only nine o'clock in the morning. This is what the prophet Joel announced would happen:

"In the Last Days," God says, "I will pour out my Spirit on every kind of people: Your sons will prophesy, also your daughters; Your young men will see visions, your old men dream dreams. When the time comes, I'll pour out my Spirit on those who serve me, men and women both, and they'll prophesy. I'll set wonders in the sky above and signs on the earth below, Blood and fire and billowing smoke, the sun turning black and the moon blood-red, Before the Day of the Lord arrives, the Day tremendous and marvelous; And whoever calls out for help to me, God, will be saved."

5. With only a pencil (or pen) use symbols, shapes and lines to create an abstract picture of what you think the crowd might have looked like (with all sorts of people) listening to Peter's speech (sermon). Label the different people-groups that you include.

   After a few minutes hold up your picture for the group to see. Describe what you drew and why.

6. During the last part of Peter's speech, he quoted a prophet (spiritual teacher) named Joel. He challenged and encouraged the crowd to join the the Jesus-mission.

   What are some thoughts of encouragement that flash into your mind as you read Peter's statement? Write them in the boxes below.

   What impact, if any, might Peter's words speak into your current life mission, if you truly believed that what he said is true?

7. Glance back through the sessions that you have experienced with this group.

   What are THREE PHRASES that you would use to summarize the most important concepts you've discovered about Jesus during these sessions?

   a. _____

   b. _____

   c. _____

ACCOUNTABLE COMMUNITY: A CELEBRATION

[If you have more than 4 or 5 people in your group, you may want to break into smaller groups for this wrap-up.]

To celebrate the time you've had together in this discussion group, have each person take a turn on "the hot seat." They may not speak.

Go around the circle until all the other group members contribute a BRIEF statement of how the person on "the hot seat" challenged them in service and helped them better understand the life of Jesus.

After each person has shared about the hot-seat person, ask one person to pray a short prayer of blessing for the "hot seat" person.

Continue around the group until everyone has had a chance on the "hot seat" and has been blessed.

Let the group leader pray a celebration and thanksgiving prayer for the entire group.

CLOSING QUESTIONS

Before the final session ends, make some decisions based on these questions:

1. Are we going to reconvene in the future, take a break (to come back when?), or move on to other things?

2. When can we have a party to celebrate the time we've been together?

3. Each of us needs to decide how we are going to continue to serve in the community and the world.

    With whom and how will I serve?

    How will we hold each other accountable?

WE SERVE TOGETHER

Between group meetings, each group member is working to serve someplace in their community. IN ADDITION, the group should be dreaming of ways they can serve together, at least once while they are together in this study.

You probably, already know a great service agency in your area. If not, check out this short list of ideas to get you started.

One or two group members will need to take the assignment to research and contact the agreed-upon agency or agencies—to arrange the best time for serving. Then others can jump in to care for the details of travel to and from the site, covering meals, childcare, needed equipment, etc.

Let this time of service be a great event, and maybe the beginning of something more long-term.

Have a great time!!!

- **Most any community has an agency that serves homeless people.** You will need to research the options and the requirements for volunteers. Look first for an agency that does more than serve meals, but that cares for the whole person. (Serving meals is important to those who are hungry, so don't discount those groups either.)

- **Give Kids the World.** If you're not from Florida, this could be a group "workcation." Or you could help a family take their special needs child to GKW.

"The Village" is a 70-acre resort complete with over 140 villa accommodations, entertainment attractions, whimsical venues, and fun specifically designed for children with special needs. Located in Kissimmee, FL, Give Kids The World has welcomed more than 100,000 families from all 50 states and over 70 countries.

Give Kids The World can offer the perfect volunteering experience for church, civic, youth and many other types of groups. They provide a fulfilling and rewarding event for your group while accomplishing needed tasks and projects at their facility. **http://www.gktw.org**

• **Look for an opportunity to work with the aging or homebound**. Many communities have agencies that you can partner with to serve this growing population group.

• **KaBOOM!** Do you know of a run-down playground or a place that really needs one? KaBOOM helps communities build playgrounds. They have contests to determine which communities receive the playgrounds and then look for volunteers to help build them. **http://kaboom.org**

• **Feeding America (formerly Second Harvest).** There are opportunities to help distribute food to those in need. Check out their website for the location nearest you. **http://feedingamerica.org**

• **Habitat for Humanity.** You can help make a huge difference in a family's life by helping to build them a home. Habitat has a long history of great service and use of volunteers. Check out the website for the location nearest you. **http://habitat.org**

GROUP LEADER NOTES

TO HELP YOU GET STARTED

FIRST!
It makes no difference if you're guiding an administrative board, a sports-bar Bible study, or something in between. Every group needs to fundtion as a community of people who live in love with one another. So the following guidelines are adaptable to any setting.

WHAT IT'S NOT
These study sessions are NOT a place for you to teach the Bible to a group of people. The PRIMARY PURPOSE of these sessions is to create healthy relationships (with God and other humans) around scripture—to connect the "3 stories" (see "A Little Group Theory," below). People will learn the Bible as it makes real connection to their lives.

AS THE LEADER
(the one who is responsible for getting the group together) Your job is not to lecture, give advice, or anything else that sounds like teaching. You're the facilitator of this group of people.

HANG ONTO YOUR CHAIR
The idea of creating a small group may be a whole new (and scary) thought for you—especially a group outside the walls of your congregation. You may have been pushed into this role by someone who gives you a paycheck. Someone may have challenged you to a stretching experiment. Or you may have been wondering how to get your ministry to a deeper level. If any

of those scenarios are true, just hang on and watch what can happen in the next few weeks.

GUIDE THE GROUP

As the team leader, you will guide the group session (topic, time usage, etc.). Keep the group on track and within the time limits, even if each question is not answered or each activity completed. It is important to give time signals (at least 5 minutes and 2 minutes) when you must cut off discussion. Every session must START and STOP on time. If some want to continue with discussion after the scheduled conclusion time, dismiss everyone and let those who want to stay, stay. This allows the group to respect those who must leave.

People will be energized for the next group session if they haven't felt trapped or been frustrated that they were just "killing time." Of course, you may hear some groans when time is cut short. Explain what you're doing—keeping your word to end the session on time. The complaining means that discussion was going well.

If you're an old pro at this small group stuff, we trust that the materials in this book will be a resource to help you move your group into a joyful and transparent community—to become a group of people who care deeply for one another and serve from that community—both with one another and to others outside the group.

PLEASE ...

- Make sure that each person has a book or printout of the week's session. Everyone should have the same scripture version. IN FACT, ask people NOT to bring other biblical commentaries, books, etc., to the group, so everyone can stay focused on the specific Bible passage and questions. Commentaries tend to shut down conversation because people believe they have the "correct answer" to questions.

- Respect each person for what they say, no matter how "off-base" it may seem.

- Set the time and place for the next group meeting.

- Care for group members and their families between meetings. That doesn't mean you do it all yourself. You encourage and coordinate (or have someone coordinate) the group members in their care of one another.

- Go FIRST in answering questions early on. It helps break the ice when you give an example of how you would answer a question.

- Break the group into 4s or 5s (try to never use 3s) for Bible study and the related questions. Then everyone will have a chance to contribute. Even the introverts who are nervous about speaking publicly will usually join in. Using 3s puts people into intimidating triangles.

- Carefully note "The Accountable Community" and "We Serve" sections near the end of each session. These are extremely important for the group's life and ministry. Details are given below.

A LITTLE GROUP THEORY

A. CONNECTING the THREE STORIES THROUGH GUIDED QUESTIONS

There are three stories that MUST connect if people are to discover what it means to be a whole person, and live in a vital, growing community. THE QUESTIONS in these sessions are intentionally worded and placed where they are to help the THREE STORIES CONNECT around the Bible.

- The FIRST story is God's story (told through the Bible) that shows God's plan to create us as amazing humans, describes our walking away from God's plan, and explains God's becoming human to call us back home to wholeness.

- The second story is another person's life story, with all its stuff.

- The third story is "my" story, with all of "my" stuff.

When the three stories come together, amazing transformation happens.

- This model of small group is built on the fact that we need to tell our story and connect that story to other people and to God.

- All of us have a child inside who wants to be released. These studies will help us "come to Jesus as a little child." So prepare to laugh and cry!

- CAUTIONS:
    1. We do NOT let people confess another person's "sins."
    2. People are only allowed to talk about their own issues.
    3. Gossip can kill a group. Often prayer requests are actu-

ally cloaked gossip. We must not allow people to talk about other people.
4. Sometimes a person may dominate conversation with their own struggles—in a specific meeting or meeting after meeting. As a leader, you may need to talk directly to such a person, in private. A group cannot do therapy for an individual. That takes special care from a professional.

- As we tell our stories in the biblical context, the scriptures will become real to us. The goal of these studies is NOT to teach the Bible as a cognitive activity, just filling people's heads with memorized content.

- While some of the questions would seem needless if we're just trying to teach Bible, **they are important for building relationships**. And there is a specific sequence to the questions.

OPEN:
The **Open** question(s) is to get the group thinking about the biblical topic in a non-threatening way; often producing laughter, bringing out positive endorphins and reducing barriers to the deeper questions that are coming.

READ & APPLY:
The **Feeling** questions (those first 2 or 3 right after the Bible reading) are very important in helping people put themselves into the scripture passage.

The next **Scripture Content** questions are just that—questions to dig out some of the content. You may want to add more questions here, but do it carefully so you don't bog down the small group or lose sight of the overall purpose. The temptation is to try to "go deeper" in study, which usually means learning facts instead of allowing the Bible to transform our lives.

Many questions are given, but you are the leader and you should know your group. Since you KNOW THE PURPOSE (above) of the various questions, feel free to rewrite or adapt the questions for your needs. HOWEVER, as you adapt, keep the flow of questions going in the right order. You'll be glad you did.

THE ACCOUNTABLE COMMUNITY:
- **Personal Application** questions are where the scripture gets personal.

- **Community Accountability** pulls everything together with the group committing themselves to stand together for each person's personal growth and the group's health.

- During this time, you have the opportunity to guide the group in caring for one another.

WE SERVE:
Each session concludes with the opportunity for group members to serve in their community. This helps build a pattern of life for each group member and moves the group outside its own circle.

B. READING THE BIBLE

It's not unusual for people to be called on to read in a group. However, it can strike terror in any introvert or person with reading difficulties. Use these guidelines when preparing to read the Bible passages together as a group.

1. Unless you know a person really well, and their reading ability, never call on a person to read "cold turkey." This is especially true when reading the Bible, which

may have difficult-to-pronounce words or complicated language structures.

2. The best way to prepare a person to read is pre-heating them before the session starts. Give them the opportunity to review the passage and plan for any difficult words or phrases.

3. If a person volunteers to read but then has difficulty getting through a passage, feel free to assist them by giving them a word or two and letting them attempt to continue.

4. Thank and compliment readers, particularly when the passage or pronunciations have been difficult.

C. A WORD ABOUT PRAYING TOGETHER

From session to session you will want to change the way the group PRAYS. Sometimes you'll want the group all together. Other weeks staying in the 4s will be best.

If you want to make your group members go "spitless" just ask them to pray out loud. But if you want to teach them to actually pray for one another, suggest various forms of prayer in a progressive way.

Level 1:
   After the group has shared concerns, you close by praying yourself.

Level 2:
   Ask for specific requests, then ask for specific volunteers to pray for those requests.

Level 3:
Ask two or three group members to volunteer to pray, then you conclude. Don't be afraid of silence for a moment or two.

Level 4:
Ask the group to sit or stand in a circle and pray out loud around the circle by saying something like, "Dear God, this is _____ . Thank you for _____. Amen." If anyone is uncomfortable with this plan, they can just say "Pass" when their turn comes.

You can also try variations of any of these, such as having the group pray silently around the circle for the person on their left.

Before long you'll have the whole group easily praying for one another. They just have to discover that it's safe to say what they're really thinking and feeling without the pressure to produce some form of "magic" words for God.

D. THE MISSION

Mission is vital to Christian growth. As a goal, each person should be serving someone else each week. The entire group should be serving together at least once each month. Of course, your group may not reach this goal right away.

However, as a leader, we can strongly encourage group members to complete the "We Serve" commitment between each session.

As for the group in mission together, see the "We Serve Together" section (p. 55) to help you get thinking about possible ways you can serve your neighborhood, city, and world.

In addition, the basic mission of the group comes in the form of an empty chair at each session. Each group member should constantly be on the lookout for friends and neighbors to fill the empty chair—to join your community of care.

It is important to plant the idea of MISSION or SERVICE at the very first gathering of the group. And continue to remind people of it each time the group meets.

E. BIRTHING NEW GROUPS

Much can be said about birthing new groups, but here are a few important guidelines.

Never use the term "split a group." Birthing is the healthy beginning of another group, out of an original group.

Once groups reach 10 to 12 people, the group needs to start planning the birth. However, "birthing" should be discussed at the very first group meeting, and every meeting thereafter, so no one is surprised.

Every group must have a group "Apprentice" as well as a "Leader." When birthing a new group, the original leader, with three to six people from the original group, leaves to start the new group. The apprentice stays to lead the original group.

Both groups must then quickly find new apprentice leaders. Birthing is easier if the original group and the newly-birthed group create a celebration party for the launch. You also might consider periodic "family reunion" parties for a couple of months.

Everyone is responsible for recruiting new group members to fill the vacancies created by the birth—and to grow the new-birthed group. Never forget the empty chair.

F. LAST BUT NOT LEAST

To be most effective in your ministry as a group leader, start seeing yourself as a pastor to your group. That's right, we said PASTOR.

Try saying that out loud to yourself:
"I am a pastor to this small group of people."

Congratulations, you did it!

You're not just a leading of meetings or the coordinator of some production. Your first role should be caring for the needs (particularly the Christian formation) of your group/team.

But before you reject the idea outright, think about it for a minute. Your congregation probably has another person you call "pastor." She or he oversees the larger ministry of the congregation. However, there is no way that one person can meet all of a congregation's many needs. The best care comes when a small group, led by its leader, takes responsibility for its team members. You are the "front-line pastor" to your "congregation."

This pastoring model may take the shape primarily of leading the small group sessions. But it should also include staying alert to the individual emotional, spiritual, etc., needs of your team members. In addition, it may mean hospital visitation or rallying the group for special support of a team member who is facing a crisis.

Here's another way to think of it: You are a COACH!

When you read that word COACH, your mind may race to indivuduals you've seen pace the sidelines of a court or field; some yelling, screaming and throwing things—others calmly watching and guiding the team.

But hundreds of years before the word COACH became a person, it was a vehicle. And that vehicle carried royalty—PRECIOUS CARGO.

Let that idea soak in your brain for a while.

Do we need to say it? When you are pastoring/coaching your group, you are carrying precious "cargo." You are helping God's Spirit move people from where they are right now to where God wants them to be, down the road.

But don't let that overwhelm you. This is God's ministry and we have the privilege of partnering with the Holy Spirit—who was at work long before you got to this place—and a team of people who can learn to care for one another.

So model care as you guide your group. Have fun watching what you and God can do together to grow your group into a wonderfully caring community!

www.ingramcontent.com/pod-product-compliance
Lightning Source LLC
LaVergne TN
LVHW021622080426
835510LV00019B/2710